Passion, Provocation & Prophecy

A Pier Paolo Pasolini Dossier

Interview by
Justin Desmangles on Pasolini
with Jack Hirschman
&
Two Arcanes by Jack Hirschman

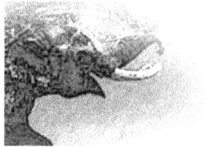

Cover Art: Self-Portrait with Scarf
(Oil on canvas)
Pier Paolo Pasolini

*"If you know that I am an unbeliever, then you know
me better than I do myself. I may be an unbeliever,
but I am an unbeliever who has a nostalgia for a
belief."*

— *Pier Paolo Pasolini*

Contents

Introduction

Before embarking on this project, I admit my knowledge of Pier Paolo Pasolini was rudimentary at best. I knew about his cinematic directions and controversial views from various undergraduate film classes but had never delved into his world in such a way that I could claim to be an expert.

I am far from an expert, but since my introduction to Jack Hirschman I have learned much about the man, the director, the poet, the prophet. I use the term prophet here, not in the mystical, but in a very concrete way. Many of his writings, his observations, and his examinations of the world around him have come to fruition in the past near 40 years since his death.

Pasolini, a major cultural figure in post WWII Italy, was a communist ousted from the Italian Communist Party for being a homosexual. He was a director and screen play writer who reformed classical roles into ones that were more reflective of humanity. For example, his production of Oedipus Rex does not create Oedipus as a sophisticated scholar, but more as an innocent observer. A characteristic far more suiting to the progress of the drama. As a rule when it came to his film direction, Pasolini attempted to recreate the story to reflect honesty. He searched for the humanity behind the role. The truth behind the propaganda.

He was not only a filmmaker, but a poet, a novelist, and he had a voice to be reckoned with. He represented a world where fascists and communists fought for power in politics and media, yet despite his controversial persona, he did not silence himself. It is his strong views and persistent writings which may have led to his ferocious assassination in 1975.

One of Pasolini's pieces which made an impact on me was the short analysis "Civil War," where Pasolini reflects on the American lifestyle through a visit to New York. In the text, he makes distinct reflections regarding the fate of the country based on the post-war mind set. The fact that many of his observations are now interwoven into American culture demonstrates just how profound and prophetic his sentiments were. He warned us of what was to come and, unheeded, our society met its predicted fate.

This book is not a collection of Pasolini's work, instead it serves as an ode to him. Beginning with an interview between Jack Hirschman and Justin Desmangles, and followed by two Arcanes written by Hirschman which reflect on the man Pasolini was, this slim edition is a companion piece to honor a voice silenced before its time.

I highly recommend adding the book *In Danger* (City Light Books, 2010) as a companion to this book. The book, edited by Jack Hirschman, is a wonderful introduction to Pasolini and his works. It includes some of his most prophetic provocations, such as "Civil War" and

"The Power Without a Face," as well as his both early and late works of poetry and several reviews. The book concludes with the last interview Pasolini conducted mere hours before his assassination.

Passion, Provocation and Prophecy is a wonderful dialogue to those who have an interest, love, understanding, and appreciation for not only Pasolini's work but for the man he was.

~Katrina K Guarascio
New Mexico 2015

"The revolution is now just a sentiment."

— *Pier Paolo Pasolini*

Jack Hirschman on Pier Paolo Pasolini
Interview with Justin Desmangles
October 15, 2010

JD: So, I was hoping to start by asking you a few questions about how Pasolini came to you. I know you've written "The Pasolini Arcane," but quotes from Pasolini's poetry have also served as epigraphs for different writings of yours as well. Where does Pasolini enter your life, personally? Where did you first encounter him as a poet, as a revolutionary?

JH: This goes back a long way, Justin, and by way of fact we're talking about an Italian poet, and here we are in the Caffe Trieste in San Francisco, where I've literally translated hundreds of poems from Italian during the years that I've lived here. But for Pasolini, that's a long story in a way. I'll try to explain it.

When I was teaching at UCLA in the '60s I wasn't so much hanging around with the folks in the English department, but I did have lunch with folks in the Italian department and the music department. And one was a writer, whose name was P.M. Pasinetti, and he'd written a book called *Venetian Red*, a novel. And one day he said, in about 1963, he said, "Have you ever heard of a poet named Pier Paolo Pasolini?" I said, "No, I hadn't."

In actual fact, I should have, and I'll tell you why. In 1958 in *Bottega Oscure*, which was an annual multi-lingual book published by Princess Caetani, Marguerita Caetani in Rome, a beautiful anthology. Pasolini appeared in the issue just prior to the one in which my, the title poem of my first book, "A Correspondence of Americans," also appeared. So I should have known, I didn't know because I didn't know Italian and his work only appeared in Italian. Years later I read the poems and I thought, wow, they're terrific poems.

Fast forward many years: actually, I started going to Italy in 1993 and I've gone there every year since then, on reading tours. Pasolini was part of the conversation of Italian poets. Why? Because as it turns out, and now with even greater hindsight, he was the most important Italian poet, not merely in the last century, I mean, I'd say for many centuries.

JD: Absolutely.

JH: Absolutely. There's no question that he was a poet who embodied high measure and fact, created great poetry. I use an acronym of his name,---in fact, I say a great poem has to have passion, provocation and prophesy---and that's PPP's, the initials of Pier Paolo Pasolini. And even though he was terribly myopic about certain things, literarily, I mean, he didn't think Pablo Neruda was a great poet. He preferred another poet, who was an old friend of mine, Ignazio Buttita, a Sicilian poet, who indeed was a very fine poet, but nowhere near the greatness, comprehensibility and depth of Pablo Neruda. But Pasolini had very strange ideas about...he didn't understand fully how important Charles Olson was to the American language. He just saw him as an imitator of Pound, which wasn't true. Pound was much closer to the English dimension even though in the radio speeches, when he was close to the American idiom, it turned out he was a fascist and an anti-semite. But in fact, Olson is the one that really broke open the American language, ie., the way Americans think on the page, as it were, or transfer energy in our language, I mean, given that the American language exists and is different from the English language.

JD: Though there is an explicit connection between Pound and Olson, to be sure.

JH: Oh yes, sure. Pound said Olson saved his life because when he was in St. Elizabeth's, Olson was the guy who came and sat with him--- until he couldn't take it anymore. I mean, after listening to that kind of anti-semitic and racist bullshit.

JD: But Pasolini's sometimes idiosyncratic point of view could be said to be a part of his nonconformity, his resistance to conformity, his willingness to give over to opinions that were certainly out of step to some degree.

JH: Well, now we're getting into who Pasolini was. I think it's very important to understand Pasolini lost his brother, who was very beloved to him: Guido was killed after the fascists were being defeated; he was killed by, actually, communists, though he was himself a communist.

He was killed by communists from the Yugoslavian partisans. They came into Northern Italy. It was a question of the territory belonging to Italy or belonging to Yugoslavia. And he was caught up in that. Pier Paolo actually joined the communist party after the war, and was the chapter head in the town of Casarsa, where he lived. Where, of course, I visited, and about which... you mentioned that I'd written "The Pasolini Arcane." But I also wrote "The Days of the Dead Arcane," which is directly about the visit to Pasolini's grave, and it's an attack on the Bush administration and the war machine, using Pasolini as the figure who speaks, as it were, from the grave.

One of my favorite odd objects I remember from his house, which is now a museum is--- on the wall, in the Friulan language, (which is not Italian, but another language that he wrote in, a the language of a northern eastern part of Italy, which includes Trieste, Veneto,--- Venice is also part of that dimension,---Udine, that language, Friulan) is an announcement Pasolini wrote in very childlike printed letters, a call for peasants and workers to get together at a public meeting. It's a beautiful object, really. It's on the wall, in a frame, in the Pasolini house-museum.

Anyway, he was busted, as you know, from the Italian Communist Party (PCI) because he was gay. But he was a very interesting homosexual. He was gay, very gay, I'm told, but he was also very conscious of homosexuality not being accepted at that point in the Party as well as by the general population. The thing about Pasolini is, rather than turn away from the class struggle, he continued to embrace it. And this is the real importance of him. because he then took a position that speaks for all those people who are not in a communist party, but who feel themselves communistically inclined.

JD: Right, that was something in particular that I felt may have been a direct influence on the development and maturity of your vision. When we think about the very well-worn question of what is the relationship of the intellectual to the revolution, Pasolini answered this by committing himself to those who would be objectively communist though they may not consider themselves to be, but also in working as an organizer and in many different artistic mediums, absolutely in the same tradition that you, as an artist, also operate. Is that something in part that you gained from your study of him? Those choices that you're making as well?

JH: Well, in a way, that certainly is part of it, no doubt about it. Some years ago, I think this was in the late '90s, 1997, I published a chapbook called *Partisans*. And in this book, I published the first essay in the anthology of Pasolini's poetry and prose, *In Danger*, that City Lights just brought out. This is the first essay in the anthology, "Civil War" translated by Susanna Bonetti. She'll be reading it at City Lights on November 3, along with Jonathan Richman, who's another translator in the book, and myself; the three of us locals are going to present some work from *In Danger*. Other translators in the book, for the record, are Giada Diano and Lucia Gazzino, both in Italy; Pasquale Verdicchio in San Diego, and Norman

MacAfee, Veruska Cantelli, and Flavio Russo in the New York area---all of them terrific translators.

In the *Partisans* chapbook, which was printed for comrades and friends that I'd met in Italy, I published a poem by Ferruccio Brugnaro, whose work I was translating. He knew Pasolini. He was a factory worker. Pasolini said that the worker-poet dimension in Italy is very important. And indeed, last year, in *Calendario*, an excellent Italian magazine, there was a whole issue devoted to the work of worker-poets. I've translated a bunch of them already. Brugnaro's work is one, Sandro Sardella is another, an extraordinary poet-painter who lives in the Varese area in northern Italy, Franco Cardinale, a Napoli factory worker. Let's put it this way: in the period of the industrial worker, some workers in factories are serious poets as well. I published *Partisans*, including their poems and my own, around "The Beautiful Banners," the poem by Pasolini that I believe contains one of the most extraordinary sections of lyrical poetry written since the end of the second world war. Allow me to read it.

I'm going to read the final section, it's a long poem; I'm just going to read the final section. Pasolini goes back through his life in "The Beautiful Banners;" he sums it up poetically from the Sixties,---he wrote it in 1962,---goes from the Sixties back through the Fifties, and he writes very autobiographically about his loves, his homosexual loves, and then he writes, and I'll read…

from THE BEAUTIFUL BANNERS

....

Slowly slowly
they've become stone monuments
that crowd my loneliness by the thousands.

Waiting
for a new wave of rationality
or a dream made in the depths of dreaming, to talk about
them.

So I wake
once again
and dress and sit at my work table.
The light of the sun already is overripe,
the peddlers further away,
the vegetable warmth more acrid in the world's markets
along inexpressibly sweet-smelling avenues,
at the edge of sea, at the feet of volcanoes.
The whole world's at work on its future epoch.

Ah! The beautiful banners of the Forties!
A pretext for a clown to weep.

But that "white" something
in Greek letters
which the dream expert irrevocably showed me
sticks to me, dressed
at the work table.
Marble, wax, or lime
on my eyelids, at the corners of my eyes:

the joyously Romanesque,
hopelessly baroque whiteness of the sun in sleep.

Real sunlight was of that whiteness
and so were the factory walls
as well as
the dust itself (on dry afternoons when
the day before was a bit rainy):
the woolen rags, the rumpled grey jackets
and frayed pants of the workers
who'd still have been able to be partisans
were of that whiteness,
as was the heat of the new springtime
oppressed by the memory of other springtimes
buried for centuries
in those very same suburbs and villages
--and ready, God,
ready to be born again
on those little walls, on those streets.

On those little walls, on those streets
steeped in strange fragrance
where the red apples and cherries flourished
in the warmth, and their red color
had a burnish to it, as
if it had been immersed in the air of a hot storm,
a red almost brown, cherries like prunes,
little apples like plums that peeped out
among the browns, intense
weft of foliage, calm, springtime was
almost in no rush,

wanted to enjoy that warmth in which the world whispered,
in its old hope, passionately of a new hope.

And over all, the waving,
the humble sluggish waving
of the red banners. God! the beautiful banners
of the Forties!
waving one after another in a mass of poor
cloth, reddening, a true red
that broke through with the dazzling destitution
of the silk covers, or the clean linen of worker families
--and with the fire of the cherries, of the apples, violet
because of the dampness, bloody because a bit of sunlight struck it,
fiery red bunched together and trembling
in the heroic tenderness of an immortal season.

(1962)

JH: That's a grand poem. That's a great lyrical moment in modern poetry.

JD: Now one of the qualities illustrated in this poem, which I find again and again in Pasolini's, his essays, his literary criticism, and obviously his poetry is the sense of momentum that one experiences when joining with the world spirit, which he defines as a revolutionary spirit, which is the whisper of spring, which is reddening the fruit, which is also the red banner and also the red flag.

That sense of openness and possibility, of this horizon meeting itself as revolution feels a part of everything that Pasolini does, no?

JH: You're absolutely correct, Justin, that's exactly it. This poem is a great fusion of nature and, mind you, this is a poem of nature, as it turns out.

JD: Similar to Lorca's sensibility with nature as well, I think.

JH: Yes. Now that we're dealing with Lorca, you'll recall Lorca was killed in 1937. This is 1962...this is 25 years later. And Pasolini takes the theme---and you know it's so apt...when I came into the Communist movement, the CLP, the Communist Labor Party, one of the things I learned early on is that dialectical materialism, the laws of dialectics, are actually true laws of the way nature is.

JD: Yes, yes. Dig it. Yes.

JH: Do you understand?

JD: Yes, absolutely.

JH: One of the reasons why I regard this poem as a great lyrical poem of the post Second World War. But I was born before the Forties and I know his accuracy in relation to those years...you know, that was when, after the Second World War, the red banners were most "pure", because Pasolini is the one as you know who prophesied the age of consumerism that would contaminate and bougeoisify the proletariat.

JD: He nailed it. He got it down.

JH: In his famous "The PCI to Young People!" and his "Apology" he took a position in favor of the cops. And he apologized for it. He took the classic Marxist position that the police were the sons and daughters of the working class, and therefore they need to be defended. And he saw the rebelling students as being the petty bourgeoisies and, in a way, he was right!

JD: He was right. In fact, I think that speaks very much to our historical moment vis-a-vis the commercialism that is strangulating, asphyxiating the image of the Beats.

JH: Yes, that's right, that's very true. These days, when I go to Italy, they call me of the Beat Generation, this after many years going there and reading in Communist halls and with comrades allover the country. But now that's changed. The Left in Italy has been deeply damaged by its capitalist class. Someone like Pasolini left a big emptiness, needless to say. Because he was also someone who made films, though I didn't include his cinema essays in the City Lights book. I just stuck to the literary and the poetic. But you know he believed that film was a language, and he used it in a way that is really quite extraordinary. And I think,--this is my personal opinion--- he made the most courageous film in the Twentieth Century, which I think *Salo* is.

JD: It's the most striking anti-fascist piece of art I've ever seen. Although, needless to say, a very difficult film to watch.

I would like to return to the poem and what we were describing, what you described so well, about the sense of the world spirit being the spirit of nature, the spirit of the horizon seeking itself as revolution, and being part of nature itself. As a theoretician, again and again we find in Pasolini that he does not speak of starting a revolution so much as joining it. That it is truly already in motion, that one aligns oneself, is moving closer to it or further away, but does not start it, from a subjective point of view. Could you comment on that, on how it's different?

JH: You're quite accurate, that is the way he was. And it has an influence on me. I'll give an example, a very clear one. Last year, the Revolutionary Poets Brigade was formed. In two weeks there'll appear a huge anthology: 300 meaty pages, 76 poets from 25 countries. The Mission Statement of the RPB is that we are poets whose weapons are our words. We want to put these words in the service of what's already in motion in society. We want to serve it, we want to serve as poets in that kind of way, so that we become involved. It's not merely just reading a poem, not like an embroidery on a bunch of speakers. We want to be part of revolutionary struggle, whether against the tyrannies vis-a-vis immigrants, against homelessness, the sit/lie situation in the city, and poems are the way we can expose the injustices. This Brigade, which started with four poets, but now at meetings at least 25 Brigadistas attend; as many at 45 will read at the Anthology readings, and RPBs have begin in Los Angeles, Albuquerque, Burlington, Vermont and Paris, France and Rome, Italy.

Here, I'm showing you, on a piece of paper, you won't be able to see it, but these are just notices. These are three different events in November [2010] only, but in December, City Lights wants to become a part of it too, so we're going to do an event with City Lights as well. These are all the poets, and we read one poem each; that's the style of the Revolutionary Poets Brigade. But we go into different areas, and serve with our poems in the struggle that's ongoing on many different fronts.

JD: And this theoretical position, or not so theoretical as practical, I should say, the practicing of this revolutionary mode of poetry seems to work very well at evading and making our way out of a lot of the problems that come from a purely subjective point of view. In other words, it liberates poetry from the kind of self-aggrandizing solipsism that sometimes we find among even those who would consider themselves progressive or revolutionary.

JH: Of course. Pasolini has another poem about "The Contemporary Literati."

JD: Right! I wanted to ask you about that particular poem. It's on page 177. When I read that poem I thought to myself, "My goodness, Jack must feel this way quite often." Perhaps you could read the poem and offer some commentary.

JH: It's a very short poem.

TO CONTEMPORARY LITERATI

I see you, you exist, we continue being friends
    happy to see and greet one another in some café
or in the homes of ironical Roman ladies.
    But our greetings, our smiles, our mutual passions
are acts in a no man's land . . . a wasteland
    for you, a border, for me between one history and the
        other.
We can't really have any rapport anymore, I fear,
    but it's what's in us that makes the world its own
        enemy.

                          (1958-59)

JH: It's a very good line, the last line of the poem, because he's speaking about the limitation of the ego that attaches itself to the notion "I am Poet, capital P" or "I am Great Writer." And that does not get beyond. Pasolini is interested in getting, as you know, to the collective, he's interested in joining what's in motion toward a new horizon.

JD: In tuning to that whisper of Spring that reddens the fruits.

JH: Exactly so. So in that way, you see, he was outside literature. In a sense, he literally was because he was also a filmmaker. But in another sense, he was very involved with the literary people, writers and new magazines. He was all that. Fortunately what his sensibility is really rooted in is the fact that he was one who early-on had joined the Italian Communist Party.

I'll tell you, this is a funny thing. I translated a book of a poet who's poetry Pasolini had read. Alfonso Gatto was from Salerno originally, where my books and *The Arcanes* are published. And Gatto played in two Pasolini movies. Pasolini liked poets, he didn't like actors, he liked natural poetical, ordinary folks. Gatto read Pasolini's early poems, as a matter of fact. The thing about Gatto is, he's not very well known in the panorama paradigm of Italian poetry. You know, for examples, Eugenio Montale, Salvatore Quasimodo and Giuseppe Ungharetti are the ones who after the Second World War became known in the United States through translations. My book was the first book of Gatto's, the one I translated, which was published by Antonieta Villamil and her Caza de Poesia of Los Angeles last year. No, the beginning of this year [2010]. But the reason for the marginalization of this great Italian poet was that Gatto had been arrested in the Thirties and spent nine months in prison for being a Communist and was writing a communist newsletter against Mussolini. That has to be seen in context. Pasolini was someone who was busted from the Communist Party, but remained a communist outside the party, and therefore for those, as I said earlier, who regard themselves as part of the communist movement but don't belong to a party, Pasolini is a very important figure. As well as being a very important figure as a poet, he was also a playwright. Once he got ill and he wrote a bunch of plays. And he was also a painter as well. And needless to say, I've tried to show some of the literary essays. He's written some incredible literary essays, with great insight, always around these points that you're bringing up too, Justin, having to do with revolution.

That's what bottoms Pasolini: the hope for a new world, a new horizon.

JD: And I wanted to return to an earlier point about the question of consumerism. We touched on it a little bit, and there's essays here about it, but Pasolini was extraordinarily prescient in what he presented as a future problem. A problem that we're in now. He seems to find consumerism in language, not just in dress, not just in the material fetish kind of culture, but also in the calcification of language. This seems to be where poetry becomes of use as a revolutionary principle. You spoke of the factory workers themselves also working as poets. But to get back to the point, Pasolini identifies consumerism and the consumer model as the replication of a single model of fascism, in essence, and a kind of calcification and moral decrepitude. Could you speak to that and the prescience here?

JH: Well, he actually believed that consumerism created fascism. He believed!

JD: He didn't make a separation, theoretically, between these things. Consumerism and fascism, to Pasolini: same thing?

JH: Yes. In effect, in this sense. If you take what Mussolini said, and use it today in our world, he said, you've got the wrong word, it's not fascism, it's corporatism. That's what it is. If you take this country now [the United States], it's corporatism which governs consumerism, governs even the government: we live in that now, we're IN that situation, and it's more and more a global phenomenon.

JD: And Pasolini saw that.

JH: And Pasolini saw that. That's where the third element is. And Italians know. I was back in Italy earlier this year, and they know. We were talking a lot about Pasolini, and "Boy," they say, "he really prophesied."

JD: He really did.

JH: He really did. He saw it back in the Sixties! And that was why he took those funny positions. I mean, I know a guy in Bologna. We were walking along, he's a compagno, a comrade, and said he could never forgive Pasolini for taking that position against the students in the Sixties. You know, I mean, think! Like here, if you were on those marches in the Sixties, you would be against the cops, you know what I mean? Because they (the cops) were attached to the war machinery.

JD: But Pasolini was playing a brilliant strategy, actually. It wasn't just a blind support. Maybe you could explain that a bit.

JH: No, of course, that's why he called it an Apology. He knew what he was doing. It's very important to know that the element of provocation in this guy is at a high level.

JD: A very high level. And always at work.

JH: That's right. And it's always intended to really wake up the sensibilities. You know, wake up sleeping sentiment. He did call the shots on consumerism. I think about what he said about its going to create a fascism, that, though it may not appear now, is going be even worse than in the Thirties,---that's how far he saw it. Now, the Thirties was pretty heavy, I mean, you've got the holocaust. But if you see how many people already, in the age of consumerism and it's global fascism, have been destroyed because the corporations have taken over the globe, and control the world.

JD: They're larger than the nations.

JH: Than the governments. There's hardly a man in congress that's not owned by the corporations.

JD: One of the things that Pasolini, in taking this position, this brilliant prophetic insight that we talk about, also integrates it into the question of sanity, where when you have fascism and the replication of society as a single model through consumerism, than this becomes the 'sane,' this becomes the superficially legit, rationalized justification. So the individual who sees, who really feels, who weeps, in this society becomes the insane, the dejected, the one who is pushed out, the tragic figure.

JH: That's why he took many diverse positions. He understood drug addicts as being the victims precisely of this dimension. They're the ones that, in effect, I use the expression from Antonin Artaud of 'suicided,' the suicided figures in society. You know that great essay--- I think it the greatest essay about an artist in the Twentieth Century, is "Van Gogh: The Man Suicided by Society." Suicided because he had some secret that society could not bear being revealed. Some special secret. What was the secret? They had the secret of revolution, that's what they have in them. Drugs is one of the ways that it's done.

But he also saw, Pasolini did, in relation to consumerism, that the fight he was engaged in was becoming completely based on immediate gratification. And therefore the hedonist dimension. Well, we see that that's so. For example, I know that the pornographization---I've written about it in many Arcanes---of the world is based in part on this relation to consumerism. You know what I mean?

JD: Absolutely.

JH: People are bought. Bought. You watch a pornographic movie, you'll find a woman, you can do anything you want, you paid five hundred dollars. That's part of what Pasolini himself was involved with. When he got into a lot of money, he was also a victim of that very thing with his gay lovers. You know, he would pay, that kind of thing. He was part of that, living in a world that is governed by consumistic corporatism, which is what we have now.

JD: So we must remain sensitive to that.

JH: Of course.

JD: And yet Pasolini is also instructing us that with these pornographies is also a kind of ideological merchandise that we're being sold.

JH: The word porn comes from the Greek word means 'whore.' Pornography is the writing about whores or the realm of whoredom, and in an age of consumerism that realm can easily be extended, metaphorically.

JD: Right. A very expansive concept in our...

JH: Of course it is. In Pasolini's sense, he was very much aware of this and you can see why I say the poem "The Beautiful Banners" is so important. Notice in that poem he goes back through three decades of himself, but in effect, he goes back through history, the history of those decades. And this is very important to him. History is a big dimension in Pasolini. And you get it especially in that poem, but you also get it in the essays.

JD: And in the poem which we referenced about the literati, where he talked about his encounter with these folks as one history encountering another. A direct reference to the philosophical idea that we see coming through Marx from Hegel about the spirit of the age, or history in essence really only being a theory, the idea of history.

JH: Exactly, exactly. Very good, yes.

JD: You know, there's also a passage in this particular poem where there seems to be a reference somewhat to the lines from Pound which he quotes back at Pound when he interviews him. Again, getting back to this particular poem about the literati. Continuing to be friends and happy to see and greet one another. There's an encounter between

Pasolini and Ezra Pound, a very complicated figure, certainly in Italy as well as the United States, where Pasolini says, we can still be friends even though we're enemies, in effect.

JH: He was really an enemy of Pound.

JD: Can you speak a little bit to that? Because you have similar encounters.

JH: I have to say I used that section largely because it had been published in the *City Lights Review* some years earlier. Otherwise, I probably wouldn't have used the section myself. But I knew of Pasolini and Pound, and Pasolini did not like Pound. He understood that he was an important figure linguistically, but he did not like him, probably for a whole bunch of reasons: One, because he was a fascist. Two, his anti-Semitism would have really riled Pasolini because Pasolini said he came from a house where religion was very naturally felt. Pasolini wrote about, especially in Friulan, the poems he wrote in Friulan, he wrote about Christ and the myth and Mary. But Pasolini said it all came from his grandmother on his mother's Susanna Colussi's side, and this grandmother was a Jewess. And I'm sure that that had to do with one of the reasons that he didn't like Pound, because Pound---don't forget, he probably heard Pound's speeches.

JD: Right, right. First hand, in real time.

JH: Yes, Pasolini probably heard them. My enmity with Pound is such that I agree you know with Olson who finally said no one who is an anti-Semite, or anti-Black, can forward writing, he only will send it into backwardness. And Pasolini, I'm sure that Pasolini felt something of the same with respect to Pound.

JD: In thinking about how one cannot move it forward without setting it backward, I think also of the idea that one must join the revolution rather than feeling one starts it.

JH: Yes, that's true. And, well of course, Pound did himself join a revolution. And it turns out that everything connected with Pound, because he was talking about, was actually in a funny way, evoking what America was becoming, in Italy. That's why he wrote that book Mussolini and/or Jefferson. You know what I mean? Because he was in Italy, not unfeeling of what was happening in America. America was becoming that kind of force. The United States that now is the leading corporationist country in the world.

JD: In thinking about the contemporary political scene, one of the things that Pasolini very courageously reminds his comrades is that in order to remain in solace with the revolution, we also have to confront our own prejudices. Despite the fact that President Barack Obama is a Christian, a nationalist, a capitalist, a neo-colonialist--- all of these things, par excellence. In fact one of the most overlooked aspects of his tenure thus far as President of the United States is that he is overseeing the largest expansion of United States military power on the African continent in the history of this country. Yet and still, we have masses of working-class people who would call themselves white, for whom, at least economically speaking, in constraints of domestic programs, are fighting against him, largely because of his race. Pasolini says that in order to be revolutionary, we have to confront our own prejudices first, to make inroads and create alliances. How do you see this playing itself out in contemporary politics, when you see the reactionary resistance against the Obama administration, despite his own Imperialist tendencies and the racism that is erupting in American life? What do you see happening?

JH: Well I have certain ambiguous responses, you know. We talked about this before, vis-a-vis Obama, and I've written, as you know, "The Urinal Stalls Arcane"---a kind of "verse-course" (discourse) with Amiri Baraka, which will be published with Amiri's litany rant, "Fight Back Against the Right Wing Attack," and the foto-montages of Theodore Harris in a book by Caza de Poesia of Los Angeles. I believe in the historical importance of the Obama election, as it turns out. But no one can undo, as far as I'm concerned, the continuation of first 80 billion dollars, and then 23 billion dollars more to continue war. War means killing women and children, not to speak of men, so I'm against it. But I will say this for Obama: I suppose the Democrats---though I'm a Communist and interested in the formation of a movement outside the two-party system---are still rapturous because the importance of the Obama election was that it created and consolidated an African-American vote that is going to be extremely difficult for the Republicans to overtake in this country in a Presidential election. That's why I say, if you ask me for my position, certainly it's outside. But I assure you the Democrats will be solidly in power again because that consolidation, which had never appeared before, at least never to such a degree that voting for a President of the United States brought in ninety-some percent of the voting population of African-Americans…. That is phenomenal. And that is not forgotten in relation to the African-American, even though there may be some who might not want to vote for Obama or the candidates he supports. But that is a huge bloc of votes. And I think it was the major precedent, as I look back on it now, of major importance, with an international resonance. He brought about a huge consolidation of a Black vote in this country.

JD: There's one other question that I wanted to ask, and sort of wrap this up. You know, we spoke about this at the beginning of this conversation in speaking about Pasolini's prescience and you mentioned the commercialization of what was an anti-commercial movement in many senses; although the Beats did not initially consider themselves to be political, naturally, of course, objectively, they were. I would like to get some of your thoughts about Allen Ginsberg's poem *Howl*, which now has been adapted into a movie and, of course, not far from here, at City Lights Books, your publisher, your friend Lawrence Ferlinghetti, *Howl* remains the best-selling title from City Lights Press.

But it seems to me that in all the folderol that is taking place in the commercial world, in the pop-cultural world, the meaning of the impact of this particular poem is completely getting lost. So I was hoping you might share some of your thoughts about, not so much necessarily what's happening in the consumer milieu, but what the meaning of this particular work by Allen Ginsberg, *Howl*, meant to you and does it, if at all, continue to stir your own poetic imagination.

JH: Of course, of course. I mean, *Howl* is the major poem of dissidence in the Cold War period. Allen was the bard of Cold War dissidence. He was an anti-war figure and ultimately found solace and satisfaction in the non-violent Buddhism that he practiced for a good part of his life. I regard the "Footnote" to *Howl* as probably one of the three or four great testaments against Imperialism that anyone has written since the end of the Second World War. There were four major political poems of literary figures after the Second World War. I'll exclude, modestly, myself. But I was brought up with three of them. One was "Thou Shalt Not," the poem that Kenneth Rexroth wrote on Dylan Thomas' death, which became really an attack ultimately on capitalism.

JD: "It was you. You and your goddamn Brooks' Brother's suit."

 JH: And then another one, which we just read only three weeks ago, one of the great poems of the twentieth century, we read it in ensemble, a comrade Gary Hicks organizing an event in Berkeley: *Let the Railsplitter Awake* by Pablo Neruda. The major, major poem of the

McCarthy witchhunt years. And the third one is the whole poem of *Howl*, but especially in the "Footnote"---ironically called a footnote---is where he really attacks the Moloch, and it's a great poem, a great anti-imperialist poem. That whole poem, which brought on so-to-speak the Beat dimension, announced in its dedication the coming to eminence of Jack Kerouac, who was---as man, poet, opener---the birth-man, who gave us the language of the African-American dimension vis-a-vis jazz, in the white world, because Allen, Jack and Lawrence were actually antennae to and of the civil rights movement that would be led by the Southern Baptist, Martin Luther King, Jr. The beatniks---and central to them was the Afro-Jewish poet Bob Kaufman as well--- were the antennae of it all. They came out of what came before in the jazz dimension. There was shmoogadoo---my word for marijuana---which was part of it, and the sort of petty bourgeois, working-class....let me put it this way....I regard…I'll always say this--I regard the greatest poem and the measure of great American poetry to be the "Song of the Open Road." I think it's the greatest poem that any American ever wrote, because it has the key to American creation. Walt asks in effect, Where does that poem come from, where's the origin of the energy of the Song? And he answers: it comes from felons. Native Americans. African-Americans. The people who are marginalized in society, that's where the energy of the society really is, the real energy, the real poetic energy.

JD: The coal in the engine.

JH: That's right, the coal in the engine, exactly. So in that sense Ginsberg's come out of that, though it's darkened, darkened by what has happened, the betrayal of the dream by the Empire of imperialism, which Allen's major work exemplifies. You remember in the "Song of the Open Road," its last two lines we've quoted in the Mission Statement of the Revolutionary Poets Brigade:

"Camerados,...will you come travel with us? Shall we stick by each other as long as we live?"

That's a call to camaraderie. And *Howl* carries that weight, and also the darkness of William Blake's satanic mills, and also the darkness of Lorca's in "The King of Harlem" poem that he wrote in New York. And don't forget that Lorca went to the same school as Allen and Jack Kerouac---Columbia University.

JD: The same school, that's right. Just a few years before, in fact. Well, thank you, so much.

JH: You're quite welcome, Justin.

"Nothing remains but to hope the end will come to extinguish the unrelenting pain of waiting for it."

— *Pier Paolo Pasolini*

The Pasolini Arcane

Homage to Pier Paolo Pasolini

1.

Do you let me live? No.
I'm continually called up, woken from my life
and asked to perform stunts for you in the world
of death you've made of things.
It's 20 years
this Day of the Dead
that the Lollobrigida woman, getting out of her car,
will have exclaimed: "Ma chi è quer fijo de mignotta
che ha scaricato 'sta monnezza sotto casa mia?
Me so detto appena l'ho visto: pareva un sacco di stracci.
E invece era n'omo. Morto."
Bloody arm twisted,
hair matted with blood,
arms blackened with bruises
and reddened with blood;
fingers of left hand
fractured and cut,
left jaw fractured,
nose flattened and bent;
ears cut in half,
the left one twisted,
wounds on shoulders,
thorax, loins;
deep laceration at nape,

wide bruise on testicles,
10 ribs and sternum broken,
liver lacerated, heart burst.

Could've been here as well, nowhere, this nowhere
I know so well, this New York of
nulla facente,
     doing nothing, or more,
for all the make-its, nothing doing
where I pass through again
lonely, old and unhappy as in my adolescence
in streets and down in cellar clubrooms,
that life of muscles turned
inside-out like a glove,
of pimples and dirty ears,
but now more immensely alone
since the making of things became
consumingly all-consuming, so that now
the naked dollar-sign is stamped
on everything and everyone
shining with darkness from depths of the greed
he warned against with a helpless innocence
(like all on this side) paradoxically indecent,
who'd also "learned to make love without love
and without remorse"
     – those two dark birds of the brain
forever preying over his body down there,
from the roof-top overhead.
The fear's really here now, endless in eyes
turning away. And stuffed into the ears. "I'm being
tortured in that building over there and no one

hears my screams!" A guitar-playing panhandler
named Pastrami on the station platform says
they've swept all the homeless away. On the train
eyes bend, read dead headlines, hands clench sheets
as a man stands in awesome shame, begging.

Yet despite this heap of deaf husks and shells,
of sounds and images, empty cups,
the projector's slowly opening, composure's
making its claim, the moil and sap of emotion
is draining away: I'm here, mid-town, Ninth Avenue
in the dark of darkness, the hustler stroll,
the same palpable danger and corruption,
corner deal, car's open window, how we picked
that one up, drove to the cellar where
the gang was waiting, and after the bitch
went down on us all, covered that weirdo
with all our spittle, withheld our bread
and chased that blowjob screaming half-naked
through the neighborhood. And now I'm here
assuming the stance of that one
20 years dead
but as if never murdered,
beaten to death, run over,
left as trash, as a whole generation
crumpled up:

He is. I lash on.
The foreskin.
In a quiet moment.

Now you've got it back again.

Him discovered alive.
His civic cheekbones,
the cut-through ribbon
of fame, the spittle.

To tear the tits of yesterday
and smash them into the mouth
of hunger.

Adam would roar.

Animals accompany him in hell.
They burn with vivid flame.
They kiss the shoulder
of his burden of bags
and the backpacks
stuffed with time.

As Greek would have it.

I know a provoker every time
I look up at greatness.

Write his mouth on and on.
He was a bright star
and after they knocked him off
the Day of the Dead
stood leaning on its bone

and a flame spurted out
of the cock of hunger.
This is 34th Street the circle
of workers in the coming and going
of the underground city who wear
the faces left after Face has been
lost swiped and stored in Technicity
the secret necropolis This is 23rd
Street where he fell where he sleeps
with the underground homeless who've
eluded recent arrests in tunnels
This is 14th Street Transfers Available
For The L Train nothing but weariness
remembered of sweat and the grime he
died in slime and slime they called
him we apotheasize *This is W. 4th Street*
Transfers For Trains All Along The Upper
Level dreaming of woods, the woodpaths,
here the night within's smackdab quit,
they're running that flag up, unfurling it,
printing it on the money, the sign that
comes out in the durndest gestures of
paint *This is a Brooklyn Bound F Train*
Step Allaway In, Thank You, eyes so
heavy-lidded, anguish pressing down on all,
the everyday rattling inside this snake
in the Apple I'll write when I get out.
Did they matter at all, the Black Jews
on soapboxes in the Eighth Avenue & 42nd
Street darkness, the only public demo down-

town? *This is York Street. J Street Will*
Be Next. Stand Clear Of The Closing Door.

2.

The only way now: clearing,
preparing for a listening
as from a delphicoracle
or Didona, "un segno della cabala
che indica Zeus",
      windlessness, stasis
being stifling now.
How bad? Bad. How worse to get? Much.
How far to go before Revolution?
Silence.
It's thing-time, the march
of naked make-it money itself,
the sort of fascism he warned
was being born in the motherless
womb

      Hearing you hearing me again.
      Si. Tu.

I concentrate on those civil
scintillations, disobediences more decent
than stars in the sky. When I thought
(but it wasn't thought I thought
and "feeling" isn't altogether accurate):
padre, it was all at once: Pasolini,
my father and, at the root of my pen,
my son David speaking to me in

the deepest places of my body,
then in the deepest place of all.

And this is the living not the dead.
Standing wide-open. Sacrificed.
The lips and meaning of the word itself.
Reincarnate ceaselessly, that
deliriously human moment fascism's
tried to deport, exile, curse, beat-down,
kick in the balls, murder in each of us
and bury under all the garbage dumped on us,
that monumental moment when nature, self
and history rise together
to the top of one's voice,
as one voice, as in the blazing fusion
at the end of his "Belle Bandiere,"
or the chorus singing Kalinka and touching
forever in the heart of that star within that's everyone's.

3.

An addio in the language of trains.
Along the river trees are walking.
In branches children are bursting into flames.
How did you get such a blazing eye could throw
such skin of loneliness around my blood
and bones? Halloween and All Saints' Day
are approaching; stir the caldron with
the stick between your legs and let the shrieks
and cackles and lamentation of the old strega
sound in the chuff and gonging as in
the sera imbarlumida di Casarsa.

The train to the rhythms non è finito...non c'è più
non è finito...non c'è più carrying addii drenched
in weeping; and with dancing devil and saints and thieves
and the Christ on stilts along the road,
his meaning takes hold, like the negation
of the negation, at the higher level
because he lived so centered in the crux of provocations
necessary to expose the infection in neo-capitalism's roots,
the circle of obsessions, the circle di merda,
the blue shit in fascism's bone,
and to reveal and foresee the hunger
and homelessness of growing millions of sottoproletari,
the attacks on immigrants,
how the overdosed and suicided and frozen young
are martyrs to a state of things,
an all-consuming consumption
sickening in its spread of nulls and voids,
its racist roots, its moral blight.
A slum kid walks along the tracks kicking a can,
looking down at his broken shoes,
gazing into the distance. He's come from a table
where gaps of emptiness are growing
day by day – spaces between words without bite.
He's listening for the memory
of that citizen of the world senza fissa dimora.

Totò's on the road as well, smiling weeping in dialect.
Sparrows and hawks encircle a garbage heap
where hungry kids are scavenging for a meal.
The litter of life by the sea.
The true litteratura of these days.

Criminals because poor, next-to-nothings, refugees
from Yugoslavia begging from cars at stoplights;
illegal Africans with items at their feet
in the marketplace, eyes flashing this way
and that, on the lookout for the cops;
ex-students jammed into a winter squat,
cheeks hollow and stubbled, complexion frayed,
eyes sunken;
post-Albanian hookers ducking in and out of doors,
or down an alley thin as a cock.

Walking the street.
His hand inside me.
È semplice.
It's rubbing the belly no one can see.
I'm pregnant with hunger and radiance.
I study. I dream.
Don't forget me.

Mouth, near the sea now, cover yourself with these
words; then the song will stand tall
and be graced by the seabirds at twilight.
They veer and dive, all dive, descending
into those eyes where images nest
and know no end of reeling.
The sponges we are, soaking up everything,
living off the offal of these leftover times.
Bring me a tumor, I'll blow
into it so its bacilli are cured of their obsession
with killing, so the body can go its way
without fear of the physical.

Because I had a pal once.
Friends I have many now.
But a pal once I had.

Let the fetuses burst in their blossoming
and the leaves burst into flames
as we walk, a Pa', through the 20
years that in a single day means the 20,
along a road strewn with
vanity, yes, but the letters!
vanity, yes, but the words, the loves,
the bodies throwing themselves
out of the vanity of the flesh
into the struggle,
for the ear finally to be done with being deaf,
for the heart to give up dying of just being a muscle.

To come to this matter of birth
standing here at the edge of the jut of your chin
monumental now along the coast up from Salerno
to Napoli and... (but which I won't make into
mythic geography...)
"who felt the cosmos on a summer night raising
an erection for the unfecund god of the living
who came on you, all the guys... like a politic
without culture, a culture without shame..."
– you –
padre filiale

Strips of sunlight across your form.
Always arriving at nowhere with spittle.
Who's shacked up with darkness across my corpse?

Can't be that train, the one that always arrives
and never parts. "You don't know
how much he gave this society, how many
he freed by collapsing himself loftily
into contradictions." Even if
the mystery of things is less and less mysterious,
and in the technology of today the blackboard
of history is being programmed to be erased,
stai, a Pa',
padre filiale,
stai.

In the end we're looking at him through a telescope
but not being murdered, brutalized, gutted, trashed,
another piece of human shit in an epoch that spares
neither the best nor the worst;
not being Who the fuck was Pasolini, and who cares?
not being that indifference crossing the deserts
in human eyes in an instant;
not even the blackward, confused, beautifully lethal
innocence of the oblivious sotto everything...

Wake up, I'm sleeping at your shoulder, wearing
my best pyjamas, being with you. Don't go, stay,
stai, I could say
but my lips are quick to do
and lose themselves in you,
and my arms are stumped like mind
before the gloriously simple tree
you pour into me a river of blazing
leaves you've become
in the heart of autumn

almost defiantly
and when I look again my eyes
are gazing out of me
from all the places in your death
these words have kissed
so that there is no you or me
but a systole/diastole of breathlessness
dying to be embodied again.

(1995)

The Days of the Dead Arcane

1.

I hope for nothing in the light of this
intrappolando in which the day on which he died,
not simply murdered, but – as with all who mean
much more than they were – like a whole nation,
even a world, –assassinated, America's voting
to re-elect a war machine to continue clubbing
and then running over entire peoples.

So here he is, one of Italy's grandest   poets,
who's lain in this grave in Casarsa, a small Friuli town,
for 29 years. Six small laurel trees over him
and Susanna Colussi, his mother, lying beside him
in touching irony. And the sound sorrow makes
when falling through itself and touching no bottom,
with its sadness of blood and its melancholy of mind
in a world out of joint, – not in the sense of not
having one between one's fingers, or sitting in a joint
and drinking away the downright injustice of these days,
but meaning that a bought and paid-for Constitution,
with a grin and gun at the nape of the world, has,
among other things, assassinated Pier Paolo Pasolini again.

2.

What serial Days of the Dead to come!
Even kid sister Marilyn, whom he poeticized so beautifully,
is in the wings shuddering on this cenotaph I'm
       constructing

of Aztec peacock feathers six feet long, photos of Marx,
        Lenin
beside a hammer and sickle flag, Mary and Joseph
and Baby Jesus too, and Jesus the Christ. And throw in
Rumi and King as well, a mountain of hair and a pyramid
of shoes. It's the pits, it's the pits,
it's the literal pits, it's the pits that rule the world.

So many dead eyes, I think there are more than
stars in the sky, and they're here too,
gathered at the tips of my forefinger and thumb
holding this pen, all the stars that died years and years
        ago.
My absentee vote's for them. And nader/nor between
two men of war. *Adda venì baffone*. Ah,there you are!
Let's have a great DeeoDee! Diodi. O diodi. *Adda venì
        baffone.*

Look at that urchin, 6 years old, a tiny accordion
in his hands, a cardboard box with nothing in it
at his squatting knees, singing on Farhadija Street
to passing crowds, and all who take notice of him
are a bank-guard who shoos him five meters away
(where he starts up again), a cop standing over him
who gets up and disappears like in a Pasolini movie.

3.

Standing naked to my waist in the hot sun
on a Baronissi balcony above Salerno, I hear
the clop of hooves, then see – beside the cars

doing their ordinary rounds in the piazza below –
13 riders on horseback, the last one a woman,
some wearing cowboy hats, one wrapped in
an American flag, heading up the street like
a posse of disciples of Bush. O Day of the Dead tomorrow,
when it's over, America, over there, over there,
where all is battery, derangement and carelessness.
What Days of the Dead ahead! Full of bodies
on so many hot corners of the world, pieces of shahid
and his (or her) victims, and the bluster and twisted tripe
palavering out of the mouths of the media:
The Gunstitution is speaking: War Vote!
Thug Vote for the gang-swarming bashes
in this desert of consumerism. Goon Vote
to keep Kill on the lips and blow away those
blowjob communist bastards. Beat 'em with 2X4s,
run 'em over with their own cars! Break into
the cowering houses, like the rain of bullets.
Between the eyes. Before they even…
Kill 'em before they reach for…and blow us
up! The Zero within the Zero's been completed.
The Left's a confirmed frog-croak, a whelp-whine.
And the Right is a dirty sun with a big black oily eye.
But Pasolini's ashes, from his burning, burning
spirit of Bestemmia under earth, Pasolini's ashes
rise on phoenix wings of flame and cry :
Bushit! Bushit! Obomber! Hunward, crasstian soldyears,
marching to the fear. In the dead of autumn
with your mugs and biers. You who bomb and kill
the very origin of Humanity, you who shred truth
and work up vulture appetites for blood in

this carrion world, soon will smell the blossom
of Victory. Its fragrance enchanting you, irresistibly.
Adoringly you'll fall to your knees to smell it
and it will oblige you by blowing up in your dead face.

(2005)

"The mark which has dominated all my work is this longing for life, this sense of exclusion, which doesn't lessen but augments this love of life."

— Pier Paolo Pasolini

About Jack Hirschman

Jack Hirschman (b. NYC, 1933) is the emeritus 4th Poet Laureate of the City of San Francisco (2006-2009). He has published or edited more than 100 books of poetry and essays, including translations from ten languages: Mayakovski (Russian), Neruda (Spanish), Artaud (French), Lombardo (Italian), Celan (German), Laraque (Haitian), Gjakova (Albanian), Gogou (Greek), Glik (Yiddish) and Nwadike (Swedish), among many others.

His own major work is *The Arcanes*, (2006) published by Multimedia Edizioni of Salerno, Italy in the American language in which the two Arcanes in this book appear. It is a 1,000 page book of his longer poems, which he calls Arcanes, and a 2nd massive volume of more than 150 new Arcanes are scheduled to be published by the same publisher in 2015.

He is a founding member of the Revolutionary Poets Brigade of San Francisco, and the World Poetry Movement in Medellin, Colombia.

About Justin Desmangles

Justin Desmangles, the current chair of the Before Columbus Foundation of Oakland, California, is one of the leading activist intellectual lights in the Bay Area. For many years as young African-American figure in the North Beach area, he organized one of the most interesting literary programs on KPOO-FM radio. No one who has ever been interviewed by Desmangles has come away from the experience without the feeling that he or she has been engaged in a discussion of both highly important, indeed revolutionary content. Among the many fortunate poets who have engaged with Desmangles in his highly charged interviews have been the late Amiri Baraka, Ishmael Reed and Will Alexander. Jazz is a bedrock aspect of Desmangles' presence in the world: he's had jazz programs on radio, and lectured on jazz as language, and now, still only in his 40s, he continues the very important work for African-American culture but also, as his insights on Pasolini reveal, for the international dimension of poetry as well.

Also available from

Swimming with Elephants Publications

Some of it is Muscle
Zachary Kluckman

Cunt.Bomb.
Jessica Helen Lopez

September
Katrina K Guarascio & Gina Marselle

Catching Calliope
A Biannual Anthology

Verbrennen
Matthew Brown

Loved Always Tomorrow
Emily Bjustrom

Heartbreak Ridge and other poems
Bill Nevins

To Anyone Who Has Ever Loved a Writer
Nika Ann

Find more titles at

swimmingwithelephants.com